P9-BID-682

OTHER HELEN EXLEY GIFTBOOKS:
To a very special Teacher

OTHER GIFTBOOKS IN THIS SERIES:

Marriage, a keepsake	For Mother, a gift of love
For my Father	Thank Heavens for Friends
Love, a celebration	To my Daughter with Love
Words of Comfort	To my Grandmother with Love

BORDER ILLUSTRATIONS BY SHARON BASSIN

Series Editor: Helen Exley.
Pictures selected by Helen Exley.
Edited by Claire Lipscomb.

Published simultaneously in 1997 by Exley Giftbooks in the
USA and Exley Publications Ltd in Great Britain.

12 11 10 9 8 7 6 5 4 3 2 1

Picture and text selection © Helen Exley 1997.
Border illustrations © Sharon Bassin 1997.
The moral right of the author has been asserted.

ISBN 1-86187-160-0

Exley Publications Ltd, 16 Chalk Hill, Watford, Herts WD1 4BN, UK.
Exley Publications LLC, 232 Madison Avenue, Suite 1206, NY 10016, USA.

Pictures researched by Image Select International.
Typeset by Delta, Watford.
Printed and bound in China.

Thank heavens for TEACHERS

A Helen Exley Giftbook

EXLEY
NEW YORK • WATFORD, UK

UNIQUE IN YOUR EYES

Here is a thank-you from all the ordinary
children you have taught – because for you
none of us was ordinary. You told us that each
of us was utterly unique – that no one quite
like us had existed since time began. That each
of us was an absolute necessity in the whole
design – a knot of gold, a flash of crimson, a
dazzle of peacock, a gentleness of green. That
we should be proud to be ourselves.

And so we are.

And walk through the world with a firmer
step – because of you.

PAM BROWN

GUARDIANS OF CIVILIZATION

Teachers are more than any other class the guardians of civilization.

BERTRAND RUSSELL

Teachers should be held in the highest honor. They are the allies of legislators; they have agency in the prevention of crime; they aid in regulating the atmosphere, whose incessant action and pressure cause the life-blood to circulate, and to return pure and healthful to the heart of the nation.

LYDIA SIGOURNEY

A liberal education is at the heart of a civil society, and at the heart of a liberal education is the act of teaching.

A. BARTLETT GIAMATTI

A load of books does not equal one good teacher.

CHINESE PROVERB

If the heavens were all parchment, and the trees of the forest all pens, and every human being were a scribe, it would be impossible to record all that I have learned from my teachers.

ATTRIBUTED TO JOHANAN BEN ZAKKAI

It is a greater work to educate a child,
in the true and larger sense of the word,
than to rule a state.

WILLIAM ELLERY CHANNING

[School principals] have powers at their
disposal with which Prime Ministers have
never yet been invested.

WINSTON CHURCHILL

What office is there which involves
more responsibility, which requires
more qualifications, and which ought,
therefore, to be more honourable, than
that of teaching?

HARRIET MARTINEAU

I AM A TEACHER.

I was born the first moment that a question
leaped from the mouth of a child.
I have been many people in many places.
I am Socrates exciting the youth of Athens to
discover new ideas through the use of questions.
I am Anne Sullivan tapping out the secrets of
the universe into the outstretched hand of
Helen Keller.
I am Aesop and Hans Christian Andersen
revealing truth through countless stories....

The names of those who have practiced my profession ring like a hall of fame for humanity... Booker T. Washington, Buddha, Confucius, Ralph Waldo Emerson, Leo Buscaglia, Moses and Jesus.

I am also those whose names and faces have long been forgotten but whose lessons and character will always be remembered in the accomplishments of their students....

I am the most fortunate of all who labor.
A doctor is allowed to usher life into the world in one magic moment. I am allowed to see that life is reborn each day with new questions, ideas and friendships.

An architect knows that if he builds with care, his structure may stand for centuries. A teacher knows that if he builds with love and truth, what he builds will last forever.

I am a warrior, daily doing battle against peer pressure, negativity, fear, conformity, prejudice, ignorance and apathy. But I have great allies: Intelligence, Curiosity, Parental Support, Individuality, Creativity, Faith, Love and Laughter all rush to my banner with indomitable support.

JOHN W. SCHLATTER

What the teacher is, is more important than
what he teaches.

KARL MENNINGER

A teacher who can arouse a feeling for one
single good action, for one single good poem,
accomplishes more than he who fills our
memory with rows on rows of natural objects,
classified with name and form.

JOHANN WOLFGANG VON GOETHE

As with all great teachers, his curriculum was
an insignificant part of what he communicated.
From him you didn't learn a subject, but life....
Tolerance and justice, fearlessness and pride,
reverence and pity, are learned in a course on
long division if the teacher has those qualities...

WILLIAM ALEXANDER PERCY

KINDNESS

My first-grade teacher was special to me because I didn't have any front teeth then and I couldn't talk that well and people used to tease me a lot. But she would stick right up for me. I still get teased about the way I talk. I wish she was still here.

FONTIA, AGE 16

My favorite teacher was my pre-one teacher. Anytime I was upset she'd cheer me up. And when we had a field trip and my mom was supposed to come but never did, my teacher said, "That's okay. I'll pretend to be your mom."

ERIN, AGE 11

One looks back with appreciation to the brilliant teachers, but with gratitude to those who touched our human feelings. The curriculum is so much necessary raw material, but the warmth is the vital element for the growing plant and for the soul of the child.

CARL JUNG

I am indebted to my father for living, but to my teacher for living well.

ALEXANDER III OF MACEDONIA

Teacher: The child's third parent.

HYMAN MAXWELL BERSTON

Teachers can change lives with just the right mix of chalk and challenges.

JOYCE A. MYERS

The more I meet and help celebrate teachers who have turned a child's attitude and achievement around, the more I grow in admiration of their day-to-day struggles and successes at capturing the attention and affection of students.

DR. ANTHONY P. WITHAM

Celebrities of all walks of life, when asked about the inspiration for their success, invariably credit a teacher. They may mention parents, coaches, directors, even their own children... but in each instance, it was "teaching" that made the difference.

JANE JOHNSON

We were an appalling bunch... too clever by half. Argumentative. Awkward. A little dangerous.

Every year we sat and waited for the door to open and our new teacher to walk in.

Every year it was Hilmore.

No one else would take us on.

For him, we would obey.

For us, he would stand against authority.

He got us through to the very end, for he could always out-think us.

But did he breathe a sigh of relief as the doors swung to behind the last of us? Or did he watch us go with a twinge of sadness... the challenge gone from his existence?

There was no one like him.

He is with us still – and will be till the day we die.

PETER GRAY

I am a teacher.
A teacher is someone who leads.
There is no magic here.
I do not walk on water,
I do not part the sea.
I just love children.

MARVA COLLINS

Teachers believe they have a gift for giving; it drives them with the same irrepressible drive that drives others to create a work of art or a market or a building.

A. Bartlett Giamatti, from "Harpers", July 1980

Teaching is the only major occupation of man for which we have not yet developed tools that make an average person capable of competence and performance. In teaching we rely on the "naturals", the ones who somehow know how to teach.

Peter Drucker

A Thanksgiving Day editorial in the newspaper told of a school teacher who asked her class of first graders to draw a picture of something they were thankful for. She thought of how little these children from poor neighborhoods actually had to be thankful for. But she knew that most of them would draw pictures of turkeys or tables with food. The teacher was taken aback with the picture Douglas handed in... a simple childishly drawn hand.

But whose hand? The class was captivated by the abstract image. "I think it must be the hand of God that brings us food," said one child. "A farmer," said another, "because he grows the turkeys." Finally when the others were at work, the teacher bent over Douglas's desk and asked whose hand it was. "It's your hand, Teacher," he mumbled.

She recalled that frequently at recess she had taken Douglas, a scrubby forlorn child by the hand. She often did that with the children. But it meant so much to Douglas.

ANONYMOUS, FROM "CHICKEN SOUP FOR THE SOUL"

AN INSPIRATION...

I am not a teacher, but an awakener.

ROBERT FROST

The true aim of every one who aspires
to be a teacher should be, not to
impart his own opinions, but
to kindle minds.

FREDERICK W. ROBERTSON

The mediocre teacher tells. The good teacher explains. The superior teacher demonstrates. The great teacher inspires.

WILLIAM ARTHUR WARD

It is the supreme art of the teacher to awaken joy in creating expression and knowledge.

ALBERT EINSTEIN

The job of a teacher is to excite in the young a boundless sense of curiosity about life, so that the growing child shall come to apprehend it with an excitement tempered by awe and wonder.

JOHN GARRETT

A young child, a fresh uncluttered mind, a world before him – to what treasures will you lead him?

GLADYS M. HUNT

In the life of every student, there's a vacuum waiting to be filled by a teacher who can impart greater self-confidence, who can nurture undiscovered talents, and who can direct untapped energies into some form of personal fulfillment.

Dr. Anthony P. Witham

Our teacher introduced us to ourselves. We learned who we were and what we wanted to be. We were no longer strangers to ourselves.

Student Tribute

A master can tell you what he expects of you. A teacher, though, awakens your own expectations.

Patricia Neal

THE LIGHT OF UNDERSTANDING

Helen Keller (1880-1968) was a deaf and blind woman famous for conquering her disabilities. With the help of her devoted teacher Anne Sullivan, Helen learnt to communicate with the outside world. In the following passage, Helen describes an exhilarating breakthrough with her teacher.

I was like an unconscious clod of earth. There was nothing in me except the instinct to eat and drink and sleep.... Then suddenly, I knew not how or where or when, my brain felt the impact of another mind, and I awoke to language, to knowledge, to love.... My teacher, Anne Mansfield Sullivan, had been with me nearly a month, and she had taught me the names of a number of objects. She put them into my hand, spelled their names on her fingers and helped me to form the letters; but I had not the faintest idea what I was doing.... One day she handed me a cup and formed the letters *w-a-t-e-r*. She says

I looked puzzled and persisted in confusing the two words, spelling *cup* for *water* and *water* for *cup*.... In despair she led me out to the ivy-covered pumphouse and made me hold the cup under the spout while she pumped. With her other hand she spelled *w-a-t-e-r* emphatically. I stood still, my whole body's attention fixed on the motions of her fingers as the cool stream flowed over my hand. All at once there was a strange stir within me – a misty consciousness, a sense of something remembered. It was as if I had come back to life after being dead. I understood that what my teacher was doing with her fingers meant that the cold something that was rushing over my hand was water, and that it was possible for me to communicate with other people by these hand signs.... That first revelation was worth all those years I had spent in dark, soundless imprisonment. That word *water* dropped into my mind like the sun in a frozen winter world.

HELEN KELLER

My heart is singing for joy this morning. A miracle has happened! The light of understanding has shone upon my little pupil's mind, and behold, all things are changed!

ANNE SULLIVAN, HELEN KELLER'S TEACHER

Learning is finding out what
you already know.
Doing is demonstrating that
you know it.
Teaching is reminding others
that they know it
just as well as you.
You are all learners,
doers, teachers.

RICHARD BACH

The teacher can consult outside of hours with his superiors or colleagues; he can get advice and talk over his difficulties. But when he goes into the classroom, shuts the door, takes the lonely seat behind the desk, and looks into the shining morning faces, then he is thrown back absolutely on himself. No power on earth can help him, and nothing can save the situation if he makes a blunder. There he needs all his resources, all his courage, and infinite patience.

WILLIAM LYON PHELPS

Teachers are expected to reach unattainable goals with inadequate tools. The miracle is that at times they accomplish this impossible task.

HAIM G. GINOT

Real teaching is patience and courage and endurance and perception. It drowns the teacher. But then, so does anything done well.

PAM BROWN

A teacher stares out each year at a different set of faces – and they stare back.

How can a human being see into minds and hearts, how can he or she discover the pain and resentment, the doubt and fear that blur those minds and hearts?

How can a teacher race ahead with those who long to learn, and yet take time to understand bewilderment, nip at the heels of stragglers, deal with the dangerous, untangle those stuck fast?

The day, the term, the year comes to an end. The faces change and change again. For all the teacher can do is often not enough.

He or she can leave, or learn to teach by rote.

Or live in hope.

As you have done.

And year after year, do more to change lives for the better than we will ever know.

Charlotte Gray

THE SHARING OF WISDOM

If you have knowledge, let others light their candles at it.

THOMAS FULLER

They realized that education was not a thing of one's own to do with what one pleases – that it was not a personal privilege to be merely enjoyed by the possessor – but a precious treasure transmitted; a sacred trust to be held, used, and enjoyed, and if possible, strengthened – then passed on to others upon the same trust.

LOUIS BRANDEIS

Teaching is arguably one of the most important professions in our society because teachers are responsible for the most treasured of all resources, the human intellect.

TONY BUZAN, FROM "THE MIND MAP BOOK"

THE LOVE OF LEARNING

When someone is taught the joy of learning, it becomes a life-long process that never stops, a process that creates a logical individual. That is the challenge and joy of teaching.

MARVA COLLINS

The object of education is to prepare the young to educate themselves throughout their lives.

ROBERT MAYNARD HUTCHINS

To teach a man how he may learn to grow independently, and for himself, is perhaps the greatest service that one person can do for another.

BENJAMIN JOWETT

The entire object of true education is
to make people not merely to do the right
things, but to enjoy them; not merely
industrious, but to love industry; not merely
learned, but to love knowledge; not merely
pure, but to love purity; not merely just, but to
hunger and thirst after justice.

JOHN RUSKIN

Prejudices, it is well known, are most difficult
to eradicate from the heart whose soil has
never been loosened or fertilized by education;
they grow there, firm as weeds among stones.

CHARLOTTE BRONTË

No one has yet fully realized the wealth of
sympathy, kindness, and generosity hidden in
the soul of a child. The effort of every true
education should be to unlock that treasure.

EMMA GOLDMAN

To me the sole hope of human salvation
lies in teaching.

GEORGE BERNARD SHAW

If you plan for a year, plant a seed. If for ten years, plant a tree. If for a hundred years, teach the people. When you sow a seed once, you will reap a single harvest. When you teach people, you will reap a hundred harvests.

KUAN CHUNG

Our good deeds as teachers are like stones cast into the pool of time. Though they themselves may disappear, their ripples extend to eternity.

AFI NOTABLE QUOTE

I touch the future, I teach.

CHRISTA MCAULIFFE

A teacher has her rewards.

A gangling youth stops her in the street.

"Remember me?"

She smiles and searches through a catalog of faces.

"Bill. Bill Hudson".

"Of course! (Bill? That spherical child who fell asleep on warmish afternoons?) I never forget."

"The Carnival of the Animals. Me, I was an elephant. Saint-Saëns. When I was seven".

He's working in a garage. Has a motorbike. Happy.

With a memory of waving trunks and music on a summer afternoon.

Pam Brown

I was fifteen and my teacher may have been in his early twenties, a poet who gave us the beauty of listening to and reading poetry that throbbed and sang. There was such test of meaning that it was a living experience which would continue to give its glow and its beauty to the whole of our lives.

Did I ever say "thank you" to him, you ask? Not really, unless this can be considered a "thank you" long, long after the happening. But that class came eager to its room, was attentive and participating, a most responsive group, and all this must have given him a sense that he was reaching the people he was teaching. That in itself must have been his reward.

CAROLINE K. SIMON, FROM "A REMEMBERED GLOW"

REMEMBERED FOR LIFE

Teachers who have plugged away at their jobs for twenty, thirty, and forty years are heroes. I suspect they know in their hearts they've done a good thing, too, and are more satisfied with themselves than most people are.

Most of us end up with no more than five or six people who remember us. Teachers have thousands of people who remember them for the rest of their lives.

ANDREW A. ROONEY

For a teacher to live forever in the heart and memory of even a single child is the best tribute of all.

AFI NOTABLE QUOTE

YOU BELIEVED IN US...

We owe you a debt we try to repay – but never
quite succeed. For you believed in us – you had
dreams for us. You flung wide doors for us and
hoped we'd have the courage to pass through.

And if we meet your pupils, grown and
changed – we talk about you with a twinge of
guilt. For most of us have drifted into very
ordinary paths – the ones you showed us
seemed so steep and the end so very distant.

But when we succeed in anything, however
small, we smile toward you. It may not be
the fabulous bouquet we meant for you – but
take these lesser flowers. With our love.

PAM BROWN

I am quite sure that in the hereafter she will take me by the hand and lead me to my proper seat.

BERNARD BARUCH,
RECALLING HIS TEACHER

Acknowledgements: The publishers are grateful for permission to reproduce copyright material. Whilst every effort has been made to trace copyright holders, the publishers would be pleased to hear from any not here acknowledged. ERIN & FONTIA: Extracts from *Teachers are Special* compiled by Nancy Burke, © 1996 Nancy Burke. Published by Park Lane Press, Random House, Inc. HELEN KELLER: Grateful acknowledgement is made to the Swedenborg Foundation for permission to reprint a portion of *Light in my Darkness*, by Helen Keller / Revised by Ray Silverman, Chrysalis Books, imprint of the Swedenborg Foundation, West Chester, copyright © 1994 by Ray Silverman. All rights reserved. CAROLINE K. SIMON: Extract from '*A Remembered Glow*' by Caroline K. Simon from *The Teacher* ed. by Morris L. Ernst, © 1967 Morris L. Ernst. Published by Prentice Hall, a division of Simon & Schuster.

Picture Credits: Exley Publications is very grateful to the following individuals and organizations for permission to reproduce their pictures: Archiv für Kunst (AKG), Art Resource (AR), Ann Ronan Picture Library (ARPL), Artworks (AW), The Bridgeman Art Library (BAL), Edimedia (EDI), Fine Art Photographic Library (FAP), Rosenthal Art Slides Inc. (R), Superstock (SS): Cover: © 1997 Antoni Vila Arrufat, *A Girl Reading*, 1937, BAL; title-page: © 1997 Timothy Easton, *The Apple Basket*, BAL; p6: © 1997 Lito Balagtas, *Gagamba*, Philippine Collection; p8: *Athenian Youth Greeting Older Man*, 5th century BC, Greece, ARPL; p10/11: Homer Winslow, *Country School*, R; p12: © 1997 Peter Fiore, *Untitled*, AW; p14: © 1997 Dora Holzhandler, *Rabbi Teaching Two Children*, BAL; p16: Heinrich Matvejevitch Maniser, *In Disgrace*, FAP; p17: Frederick Spencer, *A Still Life of Apples*, FAP; p18: © 1997 Jessie Coates, *Fourth Grade Class*, SS; p20/21: William H. Snape, *The Cottage Home*, BAL; p23: © 1997 Norman Clark, *The Art Teacher*, London, BAL; p24: Cartoon by Ape (Carlo Pellegrini), *Henry George Liddell, Dean of Christchurch, Oxford, from "Vanity Fair"*, 1875, ARPL; p26/27: Allan Rohan Crite, *School Is Out*, National Museum of American Art, AR; p29: Mary Cassatt, *Family Group Reading*, SS; p30: Elizabeth Stanhope Forbes, *School Is Out*, BAL; p32: Jan Vermeer, *The Astronomer*, AKG; p35: *Learning from Jin Xunhua*, propaganda poster from the Chinese Cultural Revolution, 1966-76, by Chinese School (20th century), Private Collection, BAL; p36: Elizabeth Jane Hill, *An Apple*, BAL; p38/39: © 1997 Stephane Poulin, *To The Glory of God*, Private Collection, BAL; p40: Carl Hertel, *Children of Germany*, AKG; p43: © 1997 Stephane Poulin, *I Am A Dreamer*, Private Collection, BAL; p45: Rodolphe Ernst, *The Lesson*, AKG; p46: Guillaume Larrue, *The Student*, EDI; p49: Angele Dubas, *The Dunce's Cap*, BAL; p51: © 1997 Timothy Easton, *The Apple Basket*, BAL; p52: Emilie Mundi, *The History Book*, EDI; p54: © 1997 Amrita Sher-Gil, *Brahmacharis*, Collection NGMA New Delhi; p57: Gerritz Van Brekelenkam, *Man Meditating*, EDI; p59: Thomas Webster, *The Frown*, BAL; p60/61: Lombrichon, *Children Walking*.